THE LITTLE BOOK OF

PRIDE

THE HISTORY, THE PEOPLE,
THE PARADES

Lewis Laney

DOG 'n' BONE

Published in 2020 by Dog 'n' Bone Books
An imprint of Ryland, Peters & Small Ltd
20–21 Jockey's Fields   341 E 116th St
London WC1R 4BW   New York, NY 10029

www.rylandpeters.com

10 9 8 7 6 5 4 3 2 1

Text © Lewis Laney 2020
Design © Dog 'n' Bone Books 2020

The author's moral rights have been asserted.
All rights reserved. No part of this publication
may be reproduced, stored in a retrieval system, or
transmitted in any form or by any means, electronic,
mechanical, photocopying, or otherwise, without the
prior permission of the publisher.

A CIP catalog record for this book is available from
the Library of Congress and the British Library.

ISBN: 978 1 912983 16 2

Printed in China

Designer: Geoff Borin
Illustrations: Shutterstock/GoodStudio;
page 23: Shutterstock/Vladimir Sviracevic; pages 81,
83, 85, 87, 95, 97, 99, 100 and 103: Shutterstock/Magi
Bagi; pages 104–105: Shutterstock/Mark Rademaker,
and page 115: Shutterstock/cammep

CONTENTS

Introduction

Homosexuality has been around for a very long time. It's been documented that the Greek poet Sappho, who lived on the island of Lesbos, was writing love letters and poems to other women in the seventh century; there are countless depictions of homoerotic love between men on Greek pottery, and, albeit in subtle subtexts, same-sex love has been written about in books and played out in theaters for hundreds of years. But this isn't a book about the history or evolution of homosexuality—that would need a much bigger space than this. This is a little book about Pride.

Pride as we know it today consists of marches, parades, festivals, and various other events that give both visibility and a voice to LGBTQ+ people around the world. In many cities, Pride is an annual occasion where LGBTQ+ people, straight allies, and supporting brands and businesses come together to celebrate the queer community.

The first Pride event I went to was wonderful. There was so much happiness and I remember being surprised at just how packed the streets were. In my teens and early twenties, I attended lots of Pride events with various family, friends, and boyfriends, and I always had a great time. However, I don't think it was until I got a little older and started learning more about queer history that I fully appreciated the meaning of Pride, and how important it is.

People wave flags and brandish placards, they dress up in wild and wonderful outfits, they dance and drink, they celebrate who they are, and they share the message #LOVEISLOVE no matter your gender or sexuality. But Pride has not always been this way. Pride started out as a riot in which the queer community fought back against oppression and against being treated as criminals with few or no rights.

It's widely acknowledged that the riots, which took place at the Stonewall Inn in New York City in June 1969, were the start of the Pride movement, and a huge turning point for gay rights.

This book will primarily cover the evolution of Pride in the twentieth and twenty-first centuries. It will explore how LGBTQ+ people expressed themselves before the Stonewall riots and the Pride marches. It will look at the beginnings of a visible Pride movement; a fight back against the societies and authorities that were forcing queer people to live in the shadows. And it will profile those who have fought for queer rights and for human rights— gay, lesbian, trans, bi, queer, and drag queen activists, as well as straight allies, who stand in solidarity with the LGBTQ+ community and use their voices and platforms to bring about change and acceptance. This little book will discuss how Pride marches have evolved, how they sometimes come under threat, and how they are now a celebration of LGBTQ+ culture and history as well as a demand for change.

And what next for Pride? Now that Pride (in much of the western world) has the backing of big corporations, celebrity names, and politicians, how should it harness that power?

I hope that this book informs you about queer history and Pride. I hope it helps you to enjoy and appreciate future (and maybe your first) Pride events to their fullest.

BEFORE PRIDE

With the hundreds (perhaps thousands) of Pride events now taking place around the world, it's easy to forget that only half a century ago there were no marches, rallies, or parades as we know them now. But that doesn't mean that the LGBTQ+ community didn't exist, and it doesn't mean that they didn't have pride in themselves or try to make their voices heard. Many queer people showed pride in different ways, often in the subtext of their work, particularly in literature and the creative arts, while some were just out and proud about who they were and who they loved, and suffered the consequences. Even before the June 1969 Stonewall riots in New York City there were individuals

and groups fighting for queer rights: for the right to hold their partner's hand in public, for the right to go to work without fear of being fired just for being gay, and for the right to buy a beer in a gay bar, dressed however they wanted, without being brutally beaten.

Polari: the Secret Queer Language

For many years in Britain up to the decriminalization of homosexuality (and somewhat beyond), there was a secret queer language called Polari. It was primarily used by gay men and was most popular in larger cities, particularly London, where there were gay underground social circles. This secret language enabled gay men to discuss various things without the wider public (or the police) knowing what they were saying.

Polari was a method of communication that was made up of various words and phrases from other languages and forms of slang, and included words that were entirely made up or simply a backward spelling of a word. As a language it used English grammar but borrowed words and phrases from Thieves' Cant—a language used hundreds of years ago by thieves, beggars, and outlaws. It also included Lingua Franca, spoken by sailors and marines, Cockney Rhyming Slang—used primarily to evade the law in England—and Romani.

Polari was created to serve the needs of those in gay subculture, and so provided words and phrases for that community's activities and values. "Lily Law" or "Hilda Handcuffs" were the names given to the police to mock them, and an attractive straight man was "NAFF" (Not Available for F*****g). Other words, such

as "bona" (good), "riah" (hair), and "zhoosh" (smarten up), allowed for vapid conversations about a person's appearance without them knowing they were being discussed.

Sadly, the use of Polari began to decline in the 1960s, when a radio show featuring comedy actor Kenneth Williams began using it, letting everyone in on the secret. While it is sad that Polari fell out of favor, particularly with younger queer people who were trying to smash down the camp stereotypes it aligned with, the positive side is that its decline is also connected with the decriminalization of homosexuality, meaning less of a need for a secret language.

Queer Rights in the UK

Homosexual acts between two consenting men (in private) were decriminalized in England and Wales in 1967, two years before the aforementioned Stonewall riots in New York City (homosexuality among men was illegal in Scotland until 1981 and until 1982 in Northern Ireland). The England and Wales decriminalization came about after more than ten years of lobbying and campaigning to change the law.

In the 1950s the police in England were particularly belligerent toward homosexuals, routinely raiding public toilets to catch men "in the act," arresting and charging them. Many men were also blackmailed, later being exposed by their blackmailers and "shopped" to the authorities.

In the mid 1950s a case involving three high-profile men (the third Baron of Beaulieu Edward Montagu, landowner Michael Pitt-Rivers, and Anglo-Canadian journalist Peter Wildeblood), brought widespread attention to the laws on homosexuality. The men were charged with "conspiracy to incite certain male persons to commit serious offences with male persons" or "buggery," and imprisoned. While Montagu and Pitt-Rivers denied the charges and denied that they were homosexuals, Wildeblood openly

admitted to his homosexuality before the court. All three men were incarcerated and while in prison Wildeblood wrote *Against the Law*, a part-memoir in which he appealed to society to become more accepting of homosexuals. His aim was to show people that the majority of homosexuals were "good homosexuals," and not "the pathetically flamboyant pansy with the flapping wrists."

Largely as a response to the publicity and uproar of the Montagu trial, the UK government set up the Wolfenden Committee to investigate and possibly reform the laws covering "homosexual offences." In 1957 it published its findings in the Wolfenden Report stating, "homosexual behavior between consenting adults in private should no longer be a criminal offence." Wildeblood's contributions as the only openly gay man to be interviewed during the examination were hugely influential. Once published, the report's recommendations received surprising support from the Archbishop of Canterbury as well as from various Members of Parliament. The Homosexual Law Reform Society was set up in 1958 with literary critic and university lecturer Tony Dyson at the helm, and with the support of many notable people, such as the philosopher Bertrand Russell, novelist and playwright J.B. Priestley, and sociologist Barbara Wootton. However, it took another nine years before homosexual acts between two consenting men were partially decriminalized (in England and Wales). The Bills were brought to the House of Lords and Commons by a Conservative government and later passed in Parliament as The Sexual Offences Act 1967 by a Labour government.

It's worth noting that all of this took place in the UK before the Stonewall riots, and it's interesting to see that it was a very different demographic of queer people who helped move gay rights forward in the USA. While Wildeblood openly proclaimed that most homosexuals were **"GOOD,"** that they would assimilate into mainstream society, and that they couldn't be spotted by the average heterosexual, it was the drag queens, transvestites, femme boys, butch dykes, and the unashamedly out and proud queer community who fought back in 1969's New York City.

#Pride

"I AM A **FRUIT LOOP** IN A WORLD OF CHEERIOS."

"G.A.Y: GOOD AS YOU!"

Queer Rights in the USA

Before the Stonewall riots, there were organizations in the USA that were working to change the law and have the rights of LGBTQ+ people recognized. One of these was the Mattachine Society, founded in 1950 in Los Angeles by Harry Hay, an outspoken member of the Communist Party.

The Mattachine Society—structured in an almost secret society-like hierarchical way, with different levels of membership available—is often overlooked in LGBTQ+ history in favor of the more radical (and dramatic) Stonewall riots. However, many argue that the work of the Mattachine Society, which included publishing a magazine and creating relationships with non-gay allies, helped to break down barriers and influence public opinion.

The society gained notable attention (along with new members and financial support) by

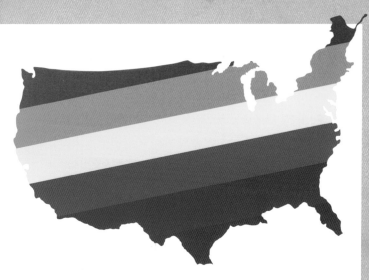

highlighting police entrapment of homosexual men when one of its members was charged with lewd behavior in a Los Angeles park. The society drummed up a lot of publicity surrounding the injustice of the case and even received support from the Citizens' Council to Outlaw Entrapment. The jury's verdict at the trial was for acquittal, citing police intimidation, harassment, and entrapment of homosexuals. This was a resounding win for the queers!

The Sip-in

The Mattachine Society had various chapters (groups) across a number of US cities and it was the New York chapter that was responsible for an act of publicity-grabbing defiance known as the "sip-in." Taking inspiration from the "sit-ins" of the civil rights movement, the sip-in consisted of a small number of Mattachine members, led by Dick Leitsch (and accompanied by a journalist and a photographer), turning up to bars in New York City, announcing to the bartenders that they were homosexuals, and then ordering a drink. (New York State liquor laws were strict at the time and an establishment could lose its license if it was judged to be a "disorderly house," and, unfortunately for the queer community, a bar serving gay people was deemed a disorderly house.) In order to highlight this unfair treatment, the men conducting the sip-in hoped that once they proclaimed their homosexuality they would be refused a drink, and this would enable Leitsch to write and complain to New York's State Licensing Agency (SLA), hopefully starting the process of having the law overturned.

The expected refusals of service did not come at the first three venues. The bar staff did not seem to care as long as they were paying customers. In the fourth venue however (ironically, a gay bar that was trying to avoid trouble), service was refused and Leitsch was able to write to the SLA and claim discrimination. The claim was initially denied, but the Commission on Human Rights got involved and the SLA eventually changed its policy, saying they no longer viewed homosexuals as "disorderly." Another great result for the queers!

The Daughters of Bilitis

Another society that campaigned for the acceptance of queer people in the 1950s and '60s was the lesbian political group Daughters of Bilitis. The organization was originally set up as a social group and an alternative way for lesbians to meet away from frequently raided lesbian and gay bars. Similar to the Mattachine Society, the Daughters of Bilitis produced a newspaper, called *The Ladder*, and held meetings where guests were invited to speak as allies or to help educate members on relevant issues.

Members of the Daughters of Bilitis joined forces with the Mattachine Society to picket Independence Hall in Philadelphia on Independence Day every year. These peaceful marches consisted of homosexuals deliberately dressed in formal clothes assigned to their biological gender, carrying signs expressing things like "15 MILLION HOMOSEXUAL

15 MILLION HOMOSEXUAL AMERICANS ASK
FOR EQUALITY, OPPORTUNITY, DIGNITY

AMERICANS ASK FOR EQUALITY, OPPORTUNITY,
DIGNITY" and "HOMOSEXUALS ASK FOR:
EQUALITY BEFORE THE LAW." These annual
pickets, lasting 90 minutes, were called "The
Reminder" as they were seen as a way to remind
the government—and the public—that thousands
of homosexuals were being denied their rights
because of their sexuality.

Going (Do)nuts in LA

A queer uprising that is not as widely reported as the Stonewall riots, which took place ten years earlier in 1959, was the Cooper Do-nuts protest. Cooper Do-nuts was a small café in downtown Los Angeles, popular with the LGBTQ+ community because of its close proximity to two gay bars. One evening in May 1959 when police tried to arrest the patrons simply for congregating at the café, the queers fought back. They threw donuts at the officers, as well as trash, coffee cups, and utensils, forcing them to retreat to their cars and call for backup. The street was shut down as the disobedience continued for many hours.

"No one in America should ever be afraid to walk down the street holding the hand of the person they love."

Barack Obama, Politician and
44th President of the United States

OSCAR WILDE

Various laws aimed at punishing homosexuality or homosexual acts have existed in Britain throughout history, and it was the law prohibiting any sexual acts between men—labeled "gross indecency"—that was used to convict the celebrated playwright Oscar Wilde in 1895.

During his university days at Oxford, Wilde was known for his flamboyant nature, his elaborate, dazzling clothing, and his quick wit. It was his entertaining character and flair for imparting knowledge and stories that landed him a job lecturing across the USA. He did this for a year, then returned to London, England, to marry Constance Lloyd, with whom he had two sons.

Wilde published *The Picture of Dorian Gray* in 1890, which was a huge success and rocketed him to stardom. He went on to write three widely revered plays, all of which were comedies that commented on and/or ridiculed elements of society and its subjects, including *Lady Windermere's Fan* (1892), *A Woman of No Importance* (1893), and *An Ideal Husband* (1895).

The tragic events of Wilde's personal life are as famous as his literary works. In the 1890s, he met and began a love affair with Lord Alfred Douglas, whom Wilde referred to as "Bosie." Despite the laws at the time, Wilde was indiscreet when it came to showing his love for Bosie and they frequently spent time together in high society, rarely hiding their affection.

At the height of his success and with two successful plays running in London's West End, Wilde tried to sue Bosie's father, the Marquess of Queensberry, for libel. The Marquess had written a note accusing Wilde of committing homosexual acts with his son, which had become public knowledge. Wilde denied the accusation, sued for libel, and lost. The case produced evidence that proved the Marquess' accusation and Wilde was thrown in jail and sentenced to two years of hard labor—a grueling and unforgiving punishment in Victorian times.

During the trial Wilde spoke of "the love that dare not speak its name." He said,

"... [it] is such a great affection of an elder for a younger man as there was between David and Jonathan, such as Plato made the very basis of his philosophy, and such as you find in the sonnets of Michelangelo and Shakespeare... It is beautiful, it is fine, it is the noblest form of affection. There is nothing unnatural about it."

This is perhaps Wilde's most open, public proclamation of what a modern-day reader would see as homosexuality.

Later in prison, with his health deteriorating and his spirit broken, Wilde wrote to the Home Secretary begging for release and claimed that his homosexuality was an illness, not a crime. He also wrote a letter to the *Daily Chronicle*, which called for urgent prison reform, particularly for the treatment of children in detention.

After his release, Wilde spent time in Italy and France, his reputation and his health in tatters. During this time, he briefly reunited with Bosie, but after another forced separation, he died in November 1900 with only his longtime friend, Robbie Ross, by his side.

Wilde did not actively fight for queer rights, however his works consistently featured undertones of same-sex love—his story *The Portrait of Mr W.H.* goes as far as to suggest that Shakespeare's sonnets were addressed to an "enigmatic" boy actor. Wilde's work, along with the unashamed, proud way he lived his life (before his imprisonment), combine to make him the most famous gay man in Victorian Britain, earning him a deserved place in Pride history.

The Sexologist from Berlin

This chapter cannot end without mentioning one final group—a group that was not in the UK or the USA, and who were doing their thing much earlier than the 1950s—and one man in particular, Magnus Hirschfeld. Hirschfeld was a Jewish physician and sexologist who lived and worked in Berlin, Germany, in the late 1800s until the early 1930s. Hirschfeld was particularly interested in (and sympathetic toward) the plight of Oscar Wilde when he was incarcerated for gross indecency in England. Hirschfeld very much believed that homosexuality was not an illness and that it should not be punishable. He also believed that many suicides among young men were caused by their struggles of not being able to be open about their sexuality.

Hirschfeld, along with a small group of others, set up

the Scientific-Humanitarian Committee in 1897 with the main aims of educating society about homosexuality and to try and repeal Paragraph 175 of the 1871 Penal code, which stated that men who had sex with men could be imprisoned for up to five years.

Hirschfeld was well respected in his field. He gave lectures and conducted research all around the world, even being fined for "propagating obscene enquiries" when he sent out sexual orientation questionnaires to 8,000 men for his studies. He published many works on the subject of homosexuality, most famously *Berlin's Third Sex* and *Homosexuality in Men and Women*, as well as setting up the world's first Institute for Sexual Science, which he later handed over to the German state. He also contributed to and starred in a film about homosexuality, which was a bold move at this time.

Hirschfeld spent much of the late 1920s and early 1930s traveling the world, conducting

research along the way and playing a major part in the World League for Sexual Reform. In 1933 while he was abroad, Hirschfeld heard that his institute in Berlin had been ransacked by the Nazis and all its papers, research, and images were burnt, along with a bust of Hirschfeld himself. Hirschfeld died in Nice, France, in 1935.

THE FIRST PRIDE
(Was a Riot)

There are many different and often conflicting stories of exactly what happened at the Stonewall Inn in the early hours of Saturday June 28, 1969. The 1995 film *Stonewall*, based on the novel by Martin Duberman and written by Rikki Beadle-Blair, opens with a line reflecting exactly that sentiment when the lead character says...

"... there's as many Stonewall stories as there are old queens in New York... and that's a lot of queens, honey. But this here tonight is my story—my legend."

What is generally agreed upon is that what did happen that night was one of, if not *the*, most radical acts of defiance from the queer community, which paved the way for huge steps forward in gay rights.

Plenty of Room at the Inn

The Stonewall Inn on Christopher Street in Greenwich Village, New York City, was a "private members bottle club" owned and operated by Tony Laurin, aka Fat Tony, in the late 1960s. It was a dark and unsanitary place, painted black to hide fire damage from its previous incarnation as a restaurant. Fat Tony ran the Inn as a bottle club to allow him to get around the state liquor laws, which specified that regular bars or clubs serving known homosexuals were disorderly houses, meaning they could have their licenses revoked. While homosexuality itself was not illegal in New York at the time, being a homosexual trying to get a drink in a bar could easily get you thrown in jail.

Bottle clubs would run under the premise that members kept their own liquor at the club and would simply be paying the staff to serve them the drinks (rather than actually paying for the drinks themselves). One of the rules of operating as a bottle club stipulated that patrons had to sign in on entry. Many customers would use false names to avoid bribery, being outed, or to evade becoming known to the police if there was a raid.

Seen at Pride

"STONEWALL WAS A **RIOT**...
NOW WE NEED A **REVOLUTION**."

"DO YOU THINK HOMOSEXUALS
ARE **REVOLTING?** YOU BET
YOUR SWEET ASS **WE ARE!**"

"IF LIZA CAN MARRY **TWO GAY MEN** WHY CAN'T I MARRY **ONE?**"

"HIP HIP HOORAY! BOTH MY SONS ARE REALLY GAY."

Many laws restricting the rights of queers (and other groups) that sprang up around this time were driven by fear of **"THE OTHER,"** which had grown in the USA due to the panic arising from the perceived threat of communism. The government and the police came down particularly harshly on groups thought to be "congregating" to discuss illegal or unpatriotic matters. This contributed to an increase in raids on gay bars and clubs in the late 1960s.

It is thought that Fat Tony would pay the police to turn a blind eye to the goings-on at the Stonewall Inn, but the bar was still occasionally raided, its takings confiscated by the police, and its patrons arrested. Precautions were taken so that in the instance of a raid the staff could minimize the damage caused. A limited amount of alcohol was kept on the premises so that there was only a small loss if any was seized. There was a strict door policy to avoid undercover cops coming in and entrapping customers—the doorman would peer through a small space in the door that slid open and judge whether a potential customer would "fit in." The doormen also had access to a switch that would turn on the main lights in the club to warn the staff and patrons that they were about to be raided. This also gave patrons time to change their clothes if what they were wearing was deemed inappropriate for their gender by law.

Drinks were often served watered down in dirty glasses at a high cost. The intention of the Stonewall Inn's owners was to make as much money from the private members' club as possible, which left the queer community—who had limited spaces to gather—open to being taken advantage of.

Despite this, the Inn was a popular place to be. One of the main attractions was that it was one of—if not the only—gay space in New York City that allowed dancing. There were two bars, a dancefloor, a jukebox, and even go-go boys, all of which was extremely appealing. Many of the other gay bars on and around Christopher Street would not allow drag queens or "street queens" in because it left them more vulnerable to having their licenses revoked, but all types of queers were welcome at Stonewall. There was room at the Inn.

The customers at the Stonewall Inn were used to raids by the police. Many were used to being beaten, thrown in the back of a police car, and taken to jail. In fact, the Inn was raided just a few days before the now-famous Stonewall riots, but it was back in business the very next day.

On Friday June 27, 1969, Judy Garland, the actress who played Dorothy in *The Wizard of Oz*, was buried, having been found dead almost a week earlier from an accidental overdose. The world mourned and so did the New York queens. Some people claim that the loss of Garland was significant to the start of the riots, in that the queer community was already in a bad mood when the police raided the Stonewall Inn. Others dispute this. Whatever is true, as the Inn patrons drank, danced, and enjoyed themselves, the hot and sticky Friday night bled into the early hours of Saturday morning and the club started to get busy.

At 1.20am the lights went on, Deputy Inspector Seymour Pine walked in with a handful of other cops and officials, and queer culture changed forever.

"My only regret about being gay is that I repressed it for so long. I surrendered my youth to the people I feared when I could have been out there loving someone. Don't make that mistake yourself. Life's too damn short."

Armistead Maupin, author of *Tales of the City*

NEED TO KNOW

Scare Drag

The queer language of the 1950s and '60s was very different to what it is now. Terms like gender non-conformist, transgender, and non-binary were not used. Names—some of which we may view as offensive today—such as Queen, Dyke, Bull-dyke, Transvestite, and Scare Drag were more common.

The term "Queens" often simply referred to gay men; "Dyke" was a more popular term for lesbians ("Bull-dyke" being lovingly reserved for a particularly masculine looking woman); "Transvestite" was generally used in the same way we would use the word "transgender" today, and "Scare Drag" usually referred to men who would dress in a way that might blur the lines between stereotypical masculine and feminine. For example, a man might wear men's jeans but put a little rouge on their cheeks and knot their t-shirt to show off their midriff.

This kind of scare drag also enabled people to get around the law that prohibited them from dressing in clothes not intended for their legally assigned birth gender. A male wearing women's clothes could be arrested for "impersonating a female" but with scare drag—by dressing somewhere between male and female—a person could very quickly pull their t-shirt down and wipe off a little bit of makeup when the police came knocking.

Gay Power!

It was unusual for the same place to be raided twice in one week, but DI Pine was apparently incensed at the amount of corruption taking place at Stonewall and the fact that his earlier raid hadn't been taken seriously by its owners. He intended to shut it down permanently this time, even going so far as to physically remove the bar from the building!

At first the raid happened as normal: the doors were sealed, the proceeds were confiscated, bar staff were arrested, and the police lined up customers to check their IDs. Some people were apparently held in the cloakroom as the police decided who to arrest and who to release with just a warning. (The irony of holding a bunch of queens in what was effectively a giant closet was probably lost on DI Pine and the other cops.) When those who were allowed to go left the bar, they didn't head home quietly as they might normally have done, but hung around outside on the street waiting for their friends and discussing how angry they were about the constant raids.

The crowd soon started to "boo" the police and to applaud their friends and fellow patrons as they were released. Many, fittingly, responded with a bow. Those who weren't released were put in the back of a police car to be taken to jail, but many were left unguarded and simply walked out.

What happened next differs according to which account you hear or read. Some say that as the police beat a young queen in the back of a car, the crowd heard what was going

on, snapped, and retaliated. Others say that an unknown lesbian (sometimes credited as being Stormé DeLarverie), while being brutally handled by the police, shouted to the crowd of queer onlookers "Why don't you do something?"—so they did. There are also accounts of a young drag or scare queen hitting a police officer with her handbag as she was manhandled by them as being the event that sparked the rebellion. There are many more accounts, and of course these multiple events could have been happening all at the same time. Whatever it was that started the riots, the reaction was monumental and unprecedented.

The crowd grew to around 500 people and they were not happy. They started surging toward the police. They shouted and booed, then started throwing coins at the officers—perhaps as a significant metaphor for the payoffs cops received from owners of some gay bars. After the coins, it was bottles and small rocks, one of

STORMÉ DELARVERIE was a lesbian of color born in the 1920s. She performed as a drag king for many years and later worked as a volunteer street patrol worker in the lesbian community. She has been referred to as the queer Rosa Parks in various pieces written about the Stonewall riots.

which smashed a window of the Inn, then the chants of "Gay Power!" began. While some queers threw whatever they could get their hands on, others set fire to trash cans, rocked cars, and blocked the streets. The police soon realized they were outnumbered and retreated into the Inn, barricaded themselves in, and called for backup.

The Stonewall Girls

Outside, people began lighting and throwing Molotov cocktails. Others headed to nearby payphones and called their friends to increase the numbers at the riot, and some called the press. One queen named Miss New Orleans, managed to uproot a parking meter (with some help), and began using it as a battering ram on the door of the Inn.

DI Pine has since said that even after seeing frontline combat while serving in the military, he had never been more scared for his life than he was during the Stonewall riots. Interestingly, he also later said in *The New York Times*, "If what I did helped gay people, then I'm glad," justifying his raids as a means to ending organized crime in New York City—and not primarily directed at the gay community.

Backup eventually came in the form of the fire department and the Tactical Police Force (TPF), who wore helmets with visors and body shields, and came brandishing batons and tear gas. As the TPF marched toward the crowds a group of queens formed a chorus line, started kicking their legs in the air, and sang,

"We are the Stonewall Girls,
we wear our hair in curls.
We wear no underwear,
we show our pubic hairs."

They faced down the approaching cops for as long as possible then ran around the block and reappeared from somewhere else, reforming their chorus line.

There are many accounts of the TPF being particularly brutal with the crowd, who they expected to back down and disperse swiftly upon their arrival. The conflict went on for hours, resulting in many injuries on both sides and 13 arrests.

As dawn broke on Christopher Street on Saturday morning, the sunlight glistened on thousands of tiny pieces of broken glass, while queens sat on the pavement, exhausted, but with a sense of triumph, knowing that something wonderful had begun.

BARBARA GITTINGS

On October 1, 2012, a small crowd of people gathered at the corner of Locust Street, Philadelphia, to celebrate the rededication of a city center block. The block, between twelfth and thirteenth street, was named "Barbara Gittings Way," after the LGBTQ+ activist of the same name, who had lived in the city for 30 years.

Gittings was an early member of the lesbian activist group, the Daughters of Bilitis (DOB), which was active for around 14 years in the 1950s and '60s. In 1958 she started the New York chapter of the organization, commuting from her home in Philadelphia to hold meetings in the city. She soon became a prominent, active member of the group and even became editor of their publication, *The Ladder*.

Gittings took part in some of the earliest known gay rights pickets, which took place at the White House and Independence Hall in Philadelphia. Gittings was instrumental in organizing the Independence Hall events, which took place every year between 1965 and 1969 (before the Stonewall riots) and were called the Annual Reminder. They began as a protest to draw attention to the fact that gay people could be legally fired from federal employment, but soon evolved into a more general reminder to

the American people that gays and lesbians did not have basic civil rights protections.

Along with Frank Kameny, Gittings campaigned tirelessly for the declassification of homosexuality as a mental disorder. She would hold protests, storm meetings of the American Psychiatric Association (APA), even working with them to organize a panel discussion on homosexuality. Gittings and Kameny even convinced a psychiatrist to appear on the panel in disguise to support their cause. In 1973 the APA formed a board to discuss the matter and eventually voted to remove the diagnosis. Gittings described the triumph brilliantly when she said,

"we were cured en masse by the psychiatrists."*

* from "The Gay Activists Who Fought the American Psychiatric Establishment."

Gitting's other lifelong passion was for books. Although not a trained librarian, she worked in libraries and with the American Library Association (ALA) to ensure queer literature was not only widely available but well classified, making it easier for people to find.

Gittings lived with her long-time partner Kay Lahusen (who, like Gittings, was an early queer activist and member of DOB) until her death in 2007. She is often referred to as "the mother of the gay rights movement."

THE RISE OF PRIDE

Keeping the
Momentum Going

The night after the Stonewall riots, the rioting started up again in Greenwich Village, New York City. The crowds gathered and took it upon themselves to close off Christopher Street, allowing only queer people into the area, demonstrating to straights what it was like to be discriminated against based on your sexuality. Cars and buses were stopped, including a cab that unknowingly turned into the area and was subjected to rocking and banging by the crowd. Unfortunately, the terrified cab driver died of a heart attack shortly after leaving the area—this was the only known death during the riots.

The Tactical Police Force (TPF) arrived, things got violent, and queer chorus lines were formed once more. Disruption continued on Sunday through to Tuesday (although on a smaller scale on weeknights). On Wednesday July 2, the *Village Voice*, the alternative periodical for Greenwich mostly considered liberal in its stance and content, published an article on the riots in which it used homophobic words like "faggots" and "faggotry." Gay activists were furious and that evening they not only gathered at the Inn to protest, but they also marched on the *Village Voice* office to vent their fury.

In the days and weeks following the riots, various groups of queer people gathered together to discuss how they could harness the energy from the current air of revolt and create a long-lasting after effect. Protests, organizations, and newsletters were popping up everywhere.

Soon after the riots ended, Craig Rodwell, a young queer activist, distributed leaflets that called upon queer people and the authorities to get corrupt owners out of gay spaces and for legally run gay bars to be opened. Depending on which accounts you read, Rodwell also had the idea to mark the riots with an annual celebration, which later manifested itself as Christopher Street Liberation Day (CSLD). CSLD is also accredited to the militant queer feminist activist Brenda Howard, who is often referred to as "The Mother of Pride" and is honored with coming up with the idea of a "Pride Week" (although a man called L. Craig Shoonmaker

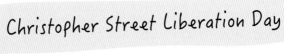

Christopher Street Liberation Day

claims to be the one to have popularized the term "Gay Pride").

Before the first CSLD march, which took place one year after the riots on June 28, 1970, and just one month after the Stonewall riots, the Mattachine Society and the Daughters of Bilitis joined forces to sponsor a march. This was largely brought about by Martha Shelley, a feminist and anti-war activist who was an active member of the New York City chapter of the Daughters of Bilitis. Shelley felt it important to keep the momentum and the spirit of the riots alive to avoid things going back to how they were before.

The first march that Shelley helped to organize took place on July 27, 1969, and consisted of hundreds of queer people marching around Greenwich Village, making speeches about how they wanted an end to police harassment and discrimination.

March for Pride

"**JESUS** HAD TWO DADS."

"BEING **STRAIGHT** WAS JUST A PHASE **I GREW OUT OF.**"

"WE ARE BOTH **THE GIRL** IN THE RELATIONSHIP. THAT'S KIND OF THE POINT."

"IF **HARRY POTTER** TAUGHT US ANYTHING, IT'S THAT NO ONE SHOULD LIVE IN A **CLOSET**."

Another successful (yet short-lived) organization that was established around this time, and of which Shelley was a founding member, was the Gay Liberation Front (GLF). The GLF was set up with the intention of being more radical than existing societies. They aligned themselves with other human rights movements like the Black Panthers and the anti-war movement. One of the group's accomplishments was the organization of regular dances for queer people. These were held at the Alternate U, a free counterculture school and leftist political center in the Village, where the queer people of New York City got to legally dance and drink at an event run by gay people, for gay people.

Sadly, the GLF did not last long. Its wish to be a radical organization created frequent divides within the group and, eventually, after a mass walkout at one of its meetings over a suggestion to make a significant donation to the Black

Panthers, it disbanded. (Other Gay Liberation Fronts were set up in 1970 in London, United Kingdom, and in Montreal, Canada.)

Other organizations that formed around this time were the Gay Activists Alliance (GAA), Street Transvestite Action Revolutionaries (STAR), formed by Marsha P. Johnson and Silvia Rivera, The Lavender Menace—later to become "Radicalesbians"—and The Christopher Street Liberation Day Committee, which eventually brought about the first large-scale political march by queer people the USA had ever seen.

One year after the Stonewall riots, queer people in New York City—and across the USA, in Chicago, Los Angeles, and San Francisco—took to the streets to celebrate who they were and to let the world know they would not hide in the shadows anymore. People kissed and held hands with their loved ones (for many this would have been the first time they felt safe to do so in public). They held signs and chanted "out of the closets and into the streets." There was no trouble or violence and the police facilitated the march as they would any other. Straight allies joined gay boys, drag queens, butch dykes, transvestites, street queens, and a whole host of other queer people, filling the streets on a march that stretched 15 blocks through New York City. Pride was born.

"If you are not personally free to be yourself in that most important of all human activities... the expression of love... then life itself loses its meaning."

Harvey Milk, Politician

MARSHA P. JOHNSON AND SILVIA RIVERA

In 2019 it was announced that Marsha P. Johnson and Silvia Rivera would be honored with a monument in New York City for the parts they played in New York's gay liberation movement of the 1960s and '70s. Until recently, both Johnson and Rivera were two little-known pioneers of queer rights in the USA.

Johnson (when asked, she said the "P" stood for "pay it no mind") was born in New Jersey and moved to New York City in 1966. Despite being a pioneering activist for trans rights and for homeless LGBTQ+ youth, Johnson's own life was a troubled one. She had several nervous breakdowns and claimed that many people had tried to kill her. Johnson's body was found in the Hudson river in July 1992, and while the cause of death was pronounced as suicide, many in the queer community believe she was murdered.

Rivera was born in New York City and was of Puerto Rican and Venezuelan descent. Orphaned at a young age, she lived temporarily with her grandmother before becoming homeless. She was later given a home by the drag queens of Greenwich Village, where she lived for the rest of her life.

Both Johnson and Rivera campaigned tirelessly for what was then referred to as transvestite rights. Together they set up the Street Transvestite Action Revolutionaries (STAR) organization to help homeless queer youth in Manhattan.

STAR

The group provided accommodation and support to those who were regarded as being on the bottom rung of the queer ladder by much of the LGBTQ+ community.

Johnson and Rivera were repeatedly incarcerated for their activism (and other crimes) and were often shunned by other members of the queer community, particularly those who wanted gay people to assimilate into mainstream society. The pair also came under fire from lesbians for wearing makeup and women's clothes. Despite all of this, they held firm to their beliefs and fought for the rights of others to live and dress how they wanted.

The monument celebrating these women is expected to be erected in Greenwich Village in 2021.

Pride Around the World

The UK

In the UK, a small rally for
gay people took place on
Highbury Fields in London
in November 1970, but

in July 1972 the first official
Gay Pride march, organized by the London arm
of the Gay Liberation Front, was held. Human
rights activist Peter Tatchell explained what Gay
Pride in London was like in 1970 in an article for
The Huffington Post: "Our aim was to show that
we were proud, not ashamed. Determined to
come out of the shadows and stand up for our
rights, we wanted to make ourselves visible and
demand LGBT liberation… Many of us saw the
Pride parade as the gay equivalent of the black
civil rights marches. We were demanding an
end to homophobia, biphobia, and transphobia.

Our slogan was 'Gay Is Good.' This simple, three-word catchphrase was revolutionary. It refuted the bigotry of centuries, which had always said that gay was mad, sad, and very, very bad."

Pride in London grew quickly, and for many years, as well as consisting of a march with political speeches, it also included a music festival, usually held in one of London's many parks. It remained a political rally, particularly in the 1980s and '90s when queer people in the UK were still fighting for their rights. In 1988 the Conservative government and Prime Minister Margaret Thatcher introduced some new legislation called Section 28, which effectively banned positive representation or discussion of homosexuality in schools. It stated that local authorities "shall not intentionally promote homosexuality or publish material with the intention of promoting homosexuality" or "promote the teaching in any maintained school of the acceptability of homosexuality as a pretended family relationship." This was a damaging piece of legislature for young queer people who required support at school or from youth services. Youth groups were closed, and teachers were restricted from offering advice and assistance.

For a number of years, many Pride marches in London focused on campaigning for the repeal of Section 28, which finally happened in 2000 in Scotland and in 2003 in the rest of the UK.

Spain

Throughout the 1970s, Pride marches began to spring up around Europe. However some countries—like Spain, where they had not even heard about Stonewall because of General Franco's dictatorship—were a little late to the party.

Spain's first Pride march took place in Barcelona in 1977 in one of the city's main streets, Las Ramblas. It was organized by Front d'Alliberament Gai de Catalunya (Gay Liberation Front of Catalonia) at a time when, despite Franco's death in 1975, laws still remained in place that discriminated against homosexuals, putting organizers and attendees at risk. The Law on Dangerousness and Social Rehabilitation (LPRS) came into force in 1970 and was used to punish and repress the Spanish LGBTQ+ community. It regarded their "crimes" on a similar level to those of vandals, drug traffickers, and prostitutes, who were also punishable under the same law. Homosexuality was finally excluded from this legislation in 1979.

Remarkably, years later in 2007, the socialist government of José Luis Rodriguez Zapatero set about compensating victims of the state who had been charged and incarcerated under such discriminatory laws.

While Spain still holds Pride events in Barcelona,

the country's biggest and most famous Pride celebrations now take place in Madrid, with more than a million people attending annually. In 2007 Madrid hosted Euro Pride and in 2017 it hosted World Pride, when it was estimated that 2.5 million people joined in the celebrations.

Brazil

In October 2018, Jair Bolsonaro, a right wing member of the Social Liberal Party, won the Presidential election in Brazil. The former military officer had once famously stated that he would rather have a dead son than a gay one. Within hours of taking office he removed responsibility for considering concerns regarding the LGBTQ+ community from a new human rights ministry, leaving such issues without a legal home.

Despite this, São Paulo Pride—which has taken place in the city since 1997—is attended by millions of people every year, and in 2019 around 3 million people took to the streets to celebrate. The event is organized by the Associação da Parada do Orgulho de Gays and Lesbicas, Bissexuais e Travestis e Transexuais (Gay and Lesbian, Bisexual, and Transvestite Pride Parade Association), and has a different slogan each year. Past slogans have included "Civil partnership now. Equal rights! Neither more nor less," "A successful country is a country without homophobia. No more deaths! Criminalization now," and "Gender identity law, now!—All people together against transphobia!"

While São Paulo Pride is regarded as the biggest Pride parade in South America, other cities including Rio de Janeiro, Belo Horizonte, and Buenos Aires also hold huge annual events.

Australia

In 1978 a group of queer
activists in California
contacted another group of
advocates thousands of miles away in Australia
to ask for their support. The Gay Freedom
Day Committee (in San Francisco) asked the
Australians if they would organize a rally in
solidarity with the opposition of an initiative
that State Senator John Briggs was planning to
put forward in California. (The Briggs initiative
would have mandated the firing of any gay or
lesbian teacher working in California's public
schools.) As a result, the Gay Solidarity Group
formed in Sydney and began to plan a march to
take place on what would become "International
Gay Solidarity Day" that June.

Despite homosexuality still being illegal
in New South Wales, the group was granted
permission to march by police, and Australia's

first Pride took place. At first the marchers were in good spirits and the event was celebratory, but as the revelers reached Hyde Park—the end of the permitted zone—the police confiscated the group's loudspeaker and truck, and things got ugly. The police arrested more than 50 people and were needlessly heavy-handed. The next day the *Sydney Morning Herald* took it upon themselves to publish the names and occupations of those arrested and this led to many LGBTQ+ people losing their jobs. The public were sympathetic, and the media was also on the side of those detained. A "drop the charges" campaign was set up, which eventually suceeded and, in addition, led to a loosening of legislation, making it easier for organizers to obtain permits for future parades.

The following year, in 1979, around 3,000 people marched in the Sydney Pride parade and there were no arrests or violence. A year later, a post-parade party element was added to the event, and in the years to come artists such as Kylie and

Dannii Minogue, Boy George, Cyndi Lauper, George Michael, and Cher would perform. The event became known as Sydney Mardi Gras, and despite various struggles throughout the years (pressure to suspend the event during the AIDS crisis and bankruptcy in the early 2000s) it quickly grew in popularity to become one of the biggest Prides in the world, attracting thousands of tourists every year.

In 1998, to celebrate the twentieth anniversary of the Sydney Mardi Gras, a group of the original participants from the first march in 1978 were called upon to lead the parade. They were named the 78ers and continue to lead the march every year.

NEED TO KNOW

The AIDS Crisis

At the end of the 1970s young healthy men in the USA began getting ill. In New York, Los Angeles, and San Francisco men were identified as suffering from sicknesses linked to compromised immune systems. In 1980 similar cases were discovered in Europe and Africa and, by June 1981, ten men were reported to have died exhibiting symptoms of Kaposi's Sarcoma, a form of cancer that causes lesions to the skin.

By 1982 more cases of this mysterious illness were being discovered in the gay community, as well as among drug users who shared needles, and hemophiliacs who were receiving blood transfusions. Initially referred to in the queer community as "Gay Cancer," scientists officially named the disease Acquired Immune Deficiency Syndrome (AIDS) and soon discovered it was caused by a virus—Human Immunodeficiency Virus (HIV)—mostly spread through sex and exposure to infected blood.

In its early days AIDS did not receive much press attention, as it was believed to affect only marginalized members of society, but as cases increased it became a wider topic for discussion and created fear among both the queer and straight communities. As patients were admitted to hospital with no known cure for their illness, they often faced homophobia and fear from medical staff. Some medical professionals would be reluctant to have physical contact with AIDS patients through concern they might catch the virus themselves. Another obstacle faced by some gay people was the right to be by their partner's side in hospital. Because gay couples had no legal recognition of their relationships, the partner (or even the friend) of a patient could be refused visitation rights if the patient's family denied them access.

These attitudes were further compounded in the USA by the fact that Ronald Reagan's Republican Government completely ignored the virus, staying silent on the issue for years. In many ways the queer community and a portion of medical professionals (primarily nurses) were left to deal with the epidemic. Ward 5B, on the fifth floor of San Francisco General Hospital, became the first facility in the country designed specifically to deal with AIDS patients in 1983. At a time when medical knowledge of the virus was minimal and death inevitable for many who contracted AIDS, the nurses on Ward 5B concentrated on care, rather than cure.

Two important responses to the AIDS crisis in the 1980s were the organizations Gay Men's Health

Crisis (GMHC) and AIDS Coalition to Unleash Power (ACT UP), both set up by the writer Larry Kramer. Early groups like these provided the support that Reagan's administration did not, but sometimes drew criticism as they primarily concentrated on caring for the sick instead of calling on the government to take action. It became common at US Pride marches throughout the 1980s to see banners and placards demanding the government pay attention to the virus and its sufferers.

In 1985 American movie star and friend of Ronald and Nancy Reagan, Rock Hudson, announced that he had AIDS. This brought widespread media attention to the issue, and many people suggest that this was a major turning point in the public's perception of the virus. They saw Hudson—a white, masculine all-American movie star—now dying of a disease they previously associated with minority groups.

In April 1987 Princess Diana of Wales opened

the United Kingdom's first purpose-built HIV/AIDS unit and made an unprecedented move of shaking the hand of a man suffering with the illness in front of the world's media. With one simple gesture the Princess showed that this was a condition that required compassion and understanding, not fear and ignorance. One month later, partly prompted by Hudson's friend Elizabeth Taylor, Reagan broke his silence and called on Americans to act with dignity and kindness to those with HIV and AIDS, and that "Final judgment is up to God."

Today, it is thought that more than 36 million people worldwide are infected with HIV. Thanks to wondrous medical science, funding, and research, it is now a manageable chronic disease, and, in recent years, the number of new infections has been decreasing in many parts of the world.

Canada

In May 1969 Canada partially
decriminalized homosexual
acts between consenting
adults (primarily led by the change of the
law concerning homosexuality in the UK).
Coincidentally, it received royal assent on June
27, 1969, one day before the Stonewall riots took
place in New York City.

Various gay rights protests, rallies, and
festivals occurred throughout the 1970s in
Canada, and in 1973 LGBTQ+ rights events took
place across the country with activities in many
cities, including Montreal, Ottawa, Vancouver,
and Winnipeg. Despite this, discrimination and
police harassment were still common.

In 1974 four lesbians were arrested in
Brunswick House, a beer hall in Toronto. The
owner took umbrage with them singing "I enjoy
being a girl," changing the word "girl" to "dyke,"

and asked them to leave. They refused and were subsequently arrested. The police treated them roughly and the women brought about charges of harassment. While the charges were later dropped due to technicalities, the incident was one of the first LGBTQ+ issues to be reported in the Canadian media and to draw attention to the discrimination against queer people.

Raids continued to take place on bars in Canada, and after protests against this in Montreal in 1977, the province of Quebec responded by passing a law to ban discrimination based on a person's sexuality. Following this, the first official Pride marches took place in Montreal and Vancouver in 1979.

In 1981 the queer community suffered more harassment when 200 police officers raided numerous bathhouses in Toronto, arresting almost 300 men in "Operation Soap." The men at the bathhouses were charged with being at or operating a "bawdy house" (brothel) and were harassed and taunted by the on-duty officers. Rallies and protests were held in response and subsequently the charges were dropped. Thirty-five years later, Toronto's police chief apologized for the raids.

East Asia

China held its first official Pride event in the city of Shanghai in 2009, but unusually, it was a Pride event without a march.

China had only decriminalized homosexuality in 1997, so it was understandable that 12 years later, the organizers of Shanghai Pride were cautious. *China Daily* reported that Tiffany Lemay, the American co-organizer of the festival, had taken legal advice on the likelihood of a street parade being allowed and was warned a request would probably not be approved.

Lemay said, "Shanghai Pride is a community-building exercise. We hope to raise awareness of issues surrounding homosexuality, raise the visibility of the gay community, help people within our community to come out, and build bridges between the gay and straight communities."

Cultural events such as film screenings and art exhibitions took place and various private parties were held in the city with a moderate estimation of around 3,000 attendees.

Taiwan Pride takes place every year in late October in Taipei, and has grown to become one of the biggest Prides in East Asia, attracting thousands of visitors from neighboring countries like Japan, South Korea, The Philippines, Thailand, Singapore, Malaysia, and Indonesia.

India

Despite India having a long
and documented history
of being open to different
types of genders, relationships, and sexualities
through Hindu and Vedic texts, the country
only decriminalized gay sex in 2018. Various
Pride marches (often with only a handful of
participants) took place before 2018, but in Delhi
in November of that year the country held its first
parade where its attendees were not marching
as criminals.

San Francisco, USA

The first San Francisco Pride parade took place in 1970, the same year CSLD began in New York City. The rainbow flag—now a recognized international symbol of the LGBTQ+ community—was first created for use at San Francisco Pride in 1978 when Harvey Milk (lovingly named "The Mayor of Castro") asked Gilbert Baker to create a visual symbol of Pride for the queer community.

The San Francisco Lesbian Gay Bisexual Transgender Pride Celebration Committee, a non-profit organization, arrange San Francisco Pride events every year and their website sfpride.org boasts that since 1997 they have "awarded over $2.5 million dollars from proceeds of the Pride Celebration and Parade to local non-profit

LGBT organizations and those organizations working on issues related to HIV/AIDS, cancer, homelessness, and animal welfare."

The city is also home to Folsom Street Fair, an annual festival catering to the fetish, leather, and BDSM community, which came about during the AIDS crisis of the 1980s when the government began shutting down bathhouses and placing restrictions on bars, limiting the places where members of the community could meet.

The Rainbow Flag

These days, if you're in a city or major town during the month of June you'd have to be walking around with your eyes closed not to notice the bounty of rainbow flags flying from shops, homes, businesses, and government buildings. A visual representation of groups and organizations showing their support for and alliance with the queer community, the rainbow flag is called many different things by various people: The Pride Rainbow Flag, The Queer Rainbow Flag, The LGBTQ+ Rainbow Flag etc., and there are many incarnations of it.

When San Franciscan queer artist Gilbert Baker first created the flag in 1978 (spurred on by Harvey Milk, who asked him to create an emblem for the queer community), he designed it with eight stripes. The original colors were hot pink, red, orange, yellow, green, turquoise, indigo, and violet, and, according to Baker, each one represented something all humans share. Pink represented sex, red was for life, orange for healing, yellow for sunlight, green for nature, turquoise for magic, indigo for serenity, and violet for the spirit.

The original eight-colored flag was sewn together by Baker and members of the San Francisco queer community and was to be flown for the first time at the San Francisco Gay Freedom Day Parade in 1978, led by Milk. Over the next few years, two colors were lost: pink was not widely available in flag fabric and was expensive to produce, and turquoise and indigo simply amalgamated to become blue.

Depending on what you read, one of the myths surrounding the creation of the rainbow flag is that it was inspired

by the song "Somewhere Over the Rainbow," sung by Judy Garland in the 1939 film *The Wizard of Oz*. Garland—long considered a gay icon—died in June 1969 and the Stonewall riots occurred the day her funeral took place later that same month.

The six-color rainbow flag is widely used across the world today, but there are multiple variations and incarnations. In recent years, a black and brown stripe has been added to the top to represent people of color in the queer community. Pastel blue, pale pink, and white—the colors of the transgender flag—have sometimes been added in an arrow formation along the left-hand side of the rainbow flag as a sign of inclusion and togetherness, but these colors can also stand alone on their own flag.

Another flag in the community is the bear flag—

made up of seven stripes, including brown, tan, black, white, and gray, with a bear paw print on the top left—representing a subculture in the LGBTQ+ community that is largely made up of men with facial and/or body hair.

There are also flags for bisexuality, made up of a thick magenta stripe at the top, a thick stripe of blue at the bottom, 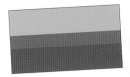 plus a thinner lavender stripe in the middle, various flags for lesbianism—the most common consisting of five colors including red, pink, and white—a flag for intersex people, which is a purple circle on a yellow background, and a flag for asexuality, which consists of four stripes: black, gray, white, and purple.

There are many more successful Pride events taking place around the world every year:

With a parade, cultural events, and a beach party, **TEL AVIV** Pride was attended by 250,000 people in 2019, making it the largest pride in the Middle East.

AMSTERDAM Pride has taken place annually since 1996, when it was created to celebrate freedom and diversity in the city. Before this, "Pink Saturday" was held in various cities in The Netherlands, the first country in the world to legalize same-sex marriage in 2001— hooray to them!

In 1979 **BERLIN** celebrated its first Christopher Street Day (CSD) with around 450 attendees. The event's name honored the original CSLD, which had taken place in New York City a decade before. The parade takes place at the end of a week-long Pride festival that includes various events. More than a million people take part annually.

South Africa only legalized sex between two men (sex between two women was never a crime) in 1998, yet the first Pride event in the country took place in 1990 in **JOHANNESBURG**. In 2012 a group of activists from the "One in Nine" feminist campaign group disrupted the parade, arguing that it had moved too far from its original political purpose and was too focused on entertainment. The organizers of Pride were divided in this matter and eventually decided to split into two groups— each aiming to organize their own separate Pride parade in the city. Johannesburg Pride is now the biggest parade in Africa with an estimated 22,000 attending in 2018.

KEEPING PRIDE
ALIVE

W hile the number of people attending Pride events is ever increasing, the parades and organizations do not exist without threats.

Protests Against Pride

Chances are that anyone who has attended a Pride event in a major city will have witnessed a counter demonstration taking place in response, but, as usual, the queer community have their own ingenious ways of fighting back.

In Atlanta in 2019, four 4 x 8-foot sound blocking panels, known as "Hate Shields," were put up in front of anti-Pride demonstrators. The shields (part funded by the Atlanta Mayor's office) not only blocked out the demonstrators visually, but they also reduced any noise they

made by around 25 percent. One other clever design feature of the Hate Shields is that they have a mirrored back, forcing the anti-Pride demonstrators to take a good, hard look at themselves while they spout their hate.

In 1999 at the trial for the killing of Matthew Shepard, a 21-year-old gay Wyoming University student who was brutally tortured, tied to a fence, and left for dead, a group of protestors turned up outside the court with anti-gay placards. In response, Shepard's friend Romaine

Patterson organized a group of people to dress as angels with huge white wings that shielded Shepard's family from the protestors. This became known as "Angel Action." A similar style of counter protest was used at some of the funerals of victims of the Pulse nightclub killings in Florida in 2016 to block anti-queer rhetoric. These simple yet effective shields allowed mourners to grieve in peace.

In 2018, Pride in London in the United Kingdom was disrupted by a group of protesters known as TERFs—trans-exclusionary radical feminists. Put simply, TERFs, who fight for women's rights, do not believe that transwomen are women and argue that they should not be allowed in women-only spaces or have the same rights and protection. The small group at London Pride obstructed the parade by laying down in front of the march and standing on the rainbow flag. Pride in London officials were unable to remove the group because their protest was not a criminal offence, so instead of letting them march in the parade, they moved them to an area in front of the procession to try and separate the two groups. Unfortunately, to many onlookers watching, it looked like this small group of TERFs was leading the parade. The next day Pride in London issued a statement denouncing the group.

"Yesterday a group of individuals... who were not a registered parade group, forced their way to the front of the parade to stand on the rainbow flag. Their behavior was shocking and disgusting, and we condemn it completely... We reject what this group stands for. They do not share our values, which are about inclusion and

respect and support for the most marginalized parts of our community. We are proud of our trans volunteers, proud of the trans groups that are in our parade, proud of our trans speakers at events, and proud of the trans people who take part in our campaigns..."

In August 2019, the same small group of people disrupted Manchester Pride.

In contrast to these two unpleasantries at Pride events, both London and Manchester are cities that proudly support and celebrate their trans communities. Sparkle: The National Transgender Charity has held "Sparkle Weekend"—a weekend of events that celebrate gender diversity and expression—in Manchester for more than 15 years. And in 2019, London's first Trans+ Pride took place in the capital, with around 1,500 people marching through the streets to show support.

"Don't accept the world as it is. Dream of what the world could be—and then help make it happen."

Peter Tatchell,
human rights activist

MADONNA

It comes as no surprise to anyone that Madonna is an ally of the queer community and adored by millions of LGBTQ+ fans around the world.

Madonna has been taken into the hearts of LGBTQ+ people not just because she's provided a soundtrack to the last 40 years of their lives, or because she is outspoken about sex, politics, and gender, but because she was one of the first stars of 1980s pop culture to speak out about gay rights and, in particular, about the AIDS crisis.

In the '80s, she hung out with the cool kids of the New York City art and music scene, many of whom were LGBTQ+. The majority of her dancers were also gay, and she was close friends with openly queer people like artist Keith Haring and comedian Sandra Bernhard.

The Queen of Pop performed at AIDS benefit concerts and spoke out about homophobia in interviews. Often questioned about her own sexuality, she once said that she doesn't bother to deny being gay when people ask her about it because "who cares?". She doesn't believe there's anything wrong with it so she's "not going to go around going 'oh God that's not true, that's not true'."

While many music artists have been accused of jumping on the bandwagon in support of LGBTQ+ issues in recent years, no one can deny that Madonna was openly supportive of the queer community long before it was deemed cool. When her critically acclaimed album, *Like a Prayer*, was released in 1989, each copy of the first run included a pamphlet about AIDS, highlighting that it was an "equal opportunities disease" and that "it affects men, women, and children, regardless of race, age, or sexual orientation."

On December 31, 2018, Madonna performed a surprise mini concert at the Stonewall Inn in New York. As well as performing "Like a Prayer," she gave a speech saying "I stand here proudly at the place where Pride began. Let us never forget the Stonewall riots and those who bravely stood up and said 'enough'." Madonna also performed at World Pride in New York City in 2019, celebrating 50 years since the Stonewall riots.

"… Since I came to New York as a wee little girl, I have always been embraced by the queer nation. I always felt like an outsider, but you made me feel like an insider. You must know how much I love and appreciate everyone here tonight—all members of the LGBTQ community. Thank you from the bottom of my heart."

Madonna

Corporate Sponsorship

There are ongoing debates in many cities that hold Pride events that the aims of the marches are being overshadowed by big corporate sponsorship, fancy floats, and entertainment. Some argue that the original meaning and purpose of Pride is being lost. As Pride grows, it attracts big names and big businesses. Many events that take place in parks and public spaces after marches (and feature music artists and other celebrities) are now paid for and ticketed, which some argue instantly excludes certain members of the queer community in lower-income brackets. Putting on parades and other events costs city councils large amounts of money and sponsorship is a way for them to recoup these expenses. Long-time human rights activist Peter Tatchell

understands the money involved, but after the 2019 Pride in London parade he stated in the *Independent* newspaper that there wasn't room for as many LGBTQ+ community groups as there should have been:

"The parade needs commercial sponsorship to fund it, but corporate floats now dominate the event... Many of the companies have degayed their floats. They don't mention LGBT+, just Pride."

In 2019, at World Pride in New York City, there was not just one march, but two. There was the regular, annual parade—arranged, as usual, by the Heritage of Pride organization—and The Queer Liberation March, set up by the Reclaim Pride Coalition. The purpose of The Queer Liberation March was to remind people of the original political purpose of Pride, and to protest the corporate sponsorship that they felt was an exploitation of the queer community. The Queer Liberation March took place with official permission from the city, but there were no corporate floats and no barriers between marchers and spectators, enabling anyone watching to join in as the parade passed by, and recreating a feeling of the original marches of the early '70s.

Sadly, some queer communities, such as those in cities like Bialystok, Poland—which saw large-scale hostility and violence at a Pride march in 2019—and Moscow City, Russia—

where the courts have banned Pride parades until 2112—can only dream of big corporate sponsorship and widespread public and political support. It's important to remember that although big businesses can often blur the main message of Pride, they do have big voices. If major corporations go on record as being open supporters of the queer community and write to the government to express this, their support can be invaluable.

Pride Power

"BLACK BY BIRTH. GAY BY GOD. PROUD BY CHOICE."

"SODOM TODAY, GOMORRAH THE WORLD."

Straight Pride... Huh?

In Boston, USA, in August 2019, a new Pride event took place: Straight Pride. It was organized by a group called Super Happy Fun America, which some newspapers claimed had links to far-right movements. Right-wing provocateur Milo Yiannopoulos headed up the parade, telling the crowd to "add the S to LGBTQ!," while attendees claimed the event was established to stand up for free speech against political correctness. In the weeks running up to the event, the organizers denied that the rally was anti-LGBTQ, but many in the queer community disputed this, arguing that its very existence was a slap in the face to the years of discrimination and persecution suffered by LGBTQ+ people.

At the Straight Pride rally, attendees spoke out against LGBTQ curriculums being taught in schools and it was apparent (from the Make America Great Again caps and the Trump-inspired float that championed the President's wall) that many of the marchers were supporters of President Donald Trump. In the summer of 2019, the Trump administration took measures to remove the rights of trans people in the workplace, prevented US Embassy buildings flying the Pride rainbow flag during Pride Month, and announced support for faith-based schools to use religion as a "right to discriminate" against queer staff as well as to remove LGBTQ+ positive curriculums in classrooms.

"I hate the word homophobia. It's not a phobia. You're not scared. You're an asshole."

Morgan Freeman, actor

It was reported that around 200 people took part in Straight Pride, however it was estimated that up to 1,000 protestors took to the streets in opposition. They flew rainbow flags and wrote positive messages in chalk on the pavements. As expected, there were clashes and more than 30 people were arrested, but the local queer community banded together again, fundraising bail for the activists who put themselves at the front of the counter protest—yet another perfect example of solidarity from LGBTQ+ people in the face of adversity.

LADY GAGA

Stefani Joanne Angelina Germanotta, or Lady Gaga as she is known to the world, has been a proud supporter of the queer community since the beginning of her career. While accepting an award for the video of her second single "Poker Face," she gave a short speech giving thanks "to God and the gays."

Lady Gaga has openly spoken out against the Trump administration's policies regarding its stance on queer people not being permitted to join the armed forces, and famously wore the "meat dress" at the 2010 MTV Video Music Awards to protest the so-called "Don't Ask Don't Tell" (DADT) policy, which prohibited any queer person from disclosing their sexual orientation while serving in the United States armed forces. Since DADT ended in 2011, people who are openly queer have been able to serve.

During the 2012 elections she recorded a special message aimed at the people of Maine, Minnesota, Washington, and Maryland, reminding them that they could vote on marriage equality at the same time as voting for their next president.

The lyrics of her 2011 single "Born This Way" seem to have been written for and about every person from a minority group:

"I'm beautiful in my way
cause God makes no mistakes
I'm on the right track, baby
I was born this way..."

The single became the fastest selling song in iTunes history and queer people around the world made it their anthem.

Gaga made a surprise appearance at the Stonewall50 commemoration in New York City in June 2019. Dressed head to toe in rainbow colors, she gave an empowering speech of support, stating how much she loved the LGBTQ+ community and that she would "take a bullet" for them. She also encouraged people to ask about a person's pronoun preference, highlighting the struggle of trans and non-binary people. She tweeted:

"This community inspires me so much. Your courage, your bravery, your relentless pursuit of kindness. Celebrate yourselves today, and hopefully every day. I love you."
—@ladygaga

Pride is Love

With Pride going on all around the world, and overseen by many different groups of people, there will always be debate about how it should be organized. There will always be opposition and those who say Pride is no longer needed, that LGBTQ+ have their rights and are recognized equally in society. While queer rights have come a long way, the fight is ongoing—and may always be—and we all need to rally together to do what we can to keep Pride alive.

Pride is still relevant. Pride is still needed. Pride still gives hope to thousands of people around the world who don't have the same rights as their straight neighbors, or who live in the shadow of a government that is taking away their freedom.

In a world where hate crimes are on the rise, Pride is love; Pride is belonging; Pride is hope; Pride is about being visible; Pride is joyous, and Pride is dancing with your community to your favorite pop star. Pride exists to create a feeling of belonging for groups of people who have felt like outsiders in the world and outsiders in their own skin.

Pride for me is best summed up in this quote from founder of Trans+ Pride in London, United Kingdom, Lucia Blayke:

"... [It's] the one day of the year trans people can stand in an open space and think: 'Wow, I'm not the outcast'."

THE PRIDE SURVIVAL GUIDE

YOUR PRIDE FLAG OF CHOICE
Whether it's blue, pink, and white or all the colors of the rainbow, fly it high and fly it proud!

WATER
You may be partaking in a celebratory drink or two throughout the day and it's more than likely you'll be out in the sun, so remember to stay hydrated.

SAFE SEX PACK
With thousands of euphoric LGBTQ+ people packed into a park, there is bound to be more than the odd suggestive gaze exchanged. Condoms, PrEP, or whatever products are best suited to you to stay safe during sex, make sure you've got them with you at Pride!

GLITTER AND FACE PAINT What member of the LGBTQ+ community doesn't want to sparkle and be a beacon of color at Pride? Just be sure your glitter is biodegradable and your face paints non-toxic.

GET WITH THE USE OF PRONOUNS Remember, there will be a lot of different members of the community out at Pride and a lot of preferred pronouns. Take a second to think about how a person might want to be addressed... and if you're not sure then use "they" or "you." If you're polite and respectful you could probably ask them which pronoun they prefer. Using the correct one could mean the difference between making a person's day or upsetting them.

I AM GAY AND I LOVE IT

PRIDE PLACARD Hopefully you're at a Pride event because you're joining the ongoing fight for equality. If so, you'll be brandishing a placard, raising a banner, or flying a flag with a queer message emblazoned on it. (Take inspiration from the ones in this book.)

COMEBACKS Despite Pride being a day when the LGBTQ+ community come together to celebrate love and fight oppression, there may be individuals who attend the marches to oppose queer rights. Some people may say mean things, and some may even have their own placards with messages of hate. These folk will be in the minority at Pride, but it's still useful to have a few comebacks ready in case you do encounter any negativity.

#LOVEWINS

It goes without saying that your retorts should be positive ones—point out all the love and happiness around you and explain that it's better to love than hate. #LOVEWINS

FRIENDS Celebrate the day with your loved ones, have fun, and look out for each other. Drink (sensibly), march, dance, and be merry! (And make sure everyone gets home safely.)

SUNSCREEN AND LIP BALM

These two don't need much explanation... you don't want to burn, and you don't want to get chapped lips, especially if you're open to a Pride kiss or two!

References
and Resources

References

Page 17: *Against the Law: The Classic Account of a Homosexual in the 1950s Britain*, (2000) Peter Wildeblood, Phoenix

Page 59: *Seymour Pine Dies at 91; Led Raid on Stonewall Inn*, Dennis Hevesi, *The New York Times*, September 7, 2010

Page 64: *The Gay Activists who Fought the American Psychiatric Establishment*, Mo Rocca, www.lithub.com, 2019

Page 81: *This is How LGBT Pride Began in 1972*, Peter Tatchell, *Huffington Post*, www.huffingtonpost.co.uk, July 7, 2017

Page 97: *Shanghai Hosts First Gay Pride Festival*, Qian Yanfeng, *China Daily*, www.chinadaily.com.cn, June 10, 2009

Page 113: *Statement from Pride in London Regarding the 2018 Protest Group*, www.prideinlondon.org, July 8, 2018

Page 121: *London Pride March Being "Degayed" by Corporate Sponsors, says Veteran Campaigner Peter Tatchell*, www.independent.co.uk, July 7, 2018

Films and books

Stonewall (1995)

Stonewall: The Riots that Sparked the Gay Revolution, (2004) David Carter, St. Martin's Press

Websites

GMHC—gmhc.org

Human Rights Campaign—hrc.org

@lgbt_history—instagram.com/lgbt_history

LGBT History Month—lgbthistorymonth.com

Making Gay History—makinggayhistory.com

Stonewall—stonewall.org.uk

The Stonewall Inn—thestonewallinnnyc.com

Terrence Higgins Trust—tht.org.uk

Index

Acknowledgments

I'd like to say a big thank you to Cindy Richards and David Peters at RPS, the publishers who liked my idea, trusted me to deliver it (a little late), and let me shape it how I saw best. But I did have help from my editors—Pete Jorgensen, Anna Galkina, and Kate Burkett—thanks for your input and for tidying up my long and messy sentences.

Shout out to Patricia Harrington in production, and the publicity and sales team at Dog 'n' Bone and Ryland Peters & Small—especially Yvonne Doolan who has had to listen to my publicity ideas for the last year.

Well done to Eliana Holder for coming up with a lovely, bright, and fresh cover that I love. Trying to create a book cover using the rainbow flag in an original way is a tough job, but she managed it. Thanks to Sally Powell and Geoff Borin for creating the design and making my text look pretty on the page!

Thanks to my family: mum and dad for 38 years of love and support, and to my sister Alex-Mary, who is my biggest ally and who has a rainbow flag constantly flying in her heart. And, of course, thanks to my partner Ben, who calms me down when I'm in a flap and is a constant source of encouragement.

And finally, I'd like to dedicate this book to two amazing people: my Nanna Jude who taught me to embrace life, "live and let live," and that mistakes make you a better person, as long as you learn from them—and who, at 83, attends Pride every year, whether I'm there or not! And, to my Auntie Mark, who marched for our rights in the '90s and helped to show me how much fun being gay can be. Not all superheroes wear capes, some of them are bald and occasionally wear size 11 high heels.